FORTNITE:
Save the World

ed.

CHERRY LAKE PUBLISHING • ANN ARBOR, MICHIGAN

by Josh Gregory

D1377451

CHERRY LAKE PRESS

Published in the United States of America by Cherry Lake Publishing
Ann Arbor, Michigan
www.cherrylakepublishing.com

Reading Adviser: Marla Conn MS, Ed., Literacy specialist, Read-Ability, Inc.

Library of Congress Cataloging-in-Publication Data
Names: Gregory, Josh, author. | Cherry Lake Publishing.
Title: Fortnite : save the world / by Josh Gregory.
Other titles: Fortnite | 21st century skills innovation library.
   Unofficial guides.
Description: Ann Arbor, Michigan : Cherry Lake Publishing, [2020] | Series:
   Unofficial guides | Includes webography. | Includes bibliographical
   references and index.
Identifiers: LCCN 2019024712 | ISBN 9781534159648 (Library Binding) |
   ISBN 9781534161948 (Paperback)
Subjects: LCSH: Fortnite Battle Royale (Game)—Juvenile literature.
Classification: LCC GV1469.35.F67 G74457 2020 | DDC 793.93–dc23
LC record available at https://lccn.loc.gov/2019024712

Cherry Lake Publishing would like to acknowledge the work of the Partnership
for 21st Century Learning, a Network of Battelle for Kids. Please visit
http://www.battelleforkids.org/networks/p21 for more information.

Printed in the United States of America
Corporate Graphics

Contents

Chapter 1

Fortnite's First Mode

When the first version of *Fortnite* was released on July 25, 2017, it was very different from the version of the game that hundreds of millions of players know and love today. The 100-player,

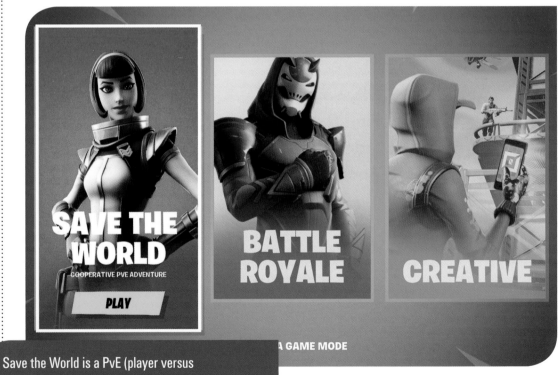

SAVE THE WORLD
COOPERATIVE PVE ADVENTURE
PLAY

BATTLE ROYALE

CREATIVE

A GAME MODE

Save the World is a PvE (player versus environment) mode, while Battle Royale is a PvP (player versus player) mode.

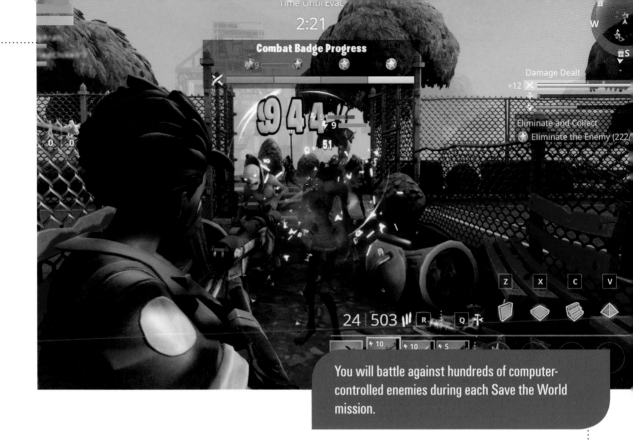

You will battle against hundreds of computer-controlled enemies during each Save the World mission.

competitive Battle Royale mode was nowhere to be found. Neither was Creative mode, which allows players to create their own *Fortnite* levels and game modes. There was only Save the World mode.

Save the World is the original *Fortnite* mode. Instead of competing against each other, Save the World players team up to defend against waves of computer-controlled enemies. To win, they need to gather supplies, **craft** useful gear, and build defensive structures.

When the game **developers** at Epic Games started working on *Fortnite* back in 2011, they wanted to create a game that focused on wilderness survival and defense. In fact, they did not start working on the Battle Royale mode at all until after Save the World was released. The two modes are closely related, though. When Epic started working on Battle Royale, they wanted to include many of Save the World's most unique features. This is why Battle Royale players have

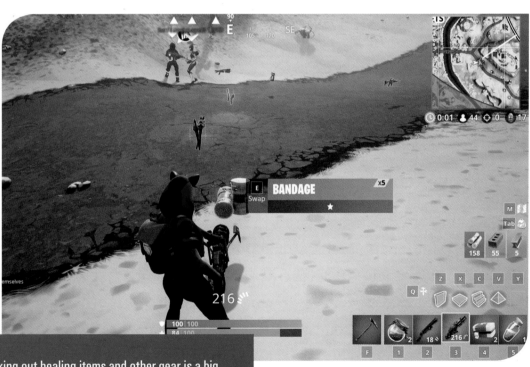

Seeking out healing items and other gear is a big part of both Battle Royale and Save the World.

Building in Save the World is almost exactly like building in Battle Royale.

to **scavenge** for gear, gather materials, and master the art of building.

While Battle Royale has become the most popular mode of *Fortnite*, Save the World still has a lot of fans. This is because it's a lot of fun! If you like the fast-paced action and strategic building of Battle Royale, you will probably enjoy Save the World as well. Many of the weapons and other gear are the same in both modes. The building system also works pretty much the same way, and you shouldn't have any trouble learning the controls of one mode if you've played the other. However, Save the World still has a lot of unique features that set it apart from Battle Royale. It is a much more complex version of *Fortnite*, and there is a lot to keep track of as you play. For example, there are countless things to collect, build, and craft. And almost every item or character you come across can be **upgraded**. If you are new to Save the World, it can

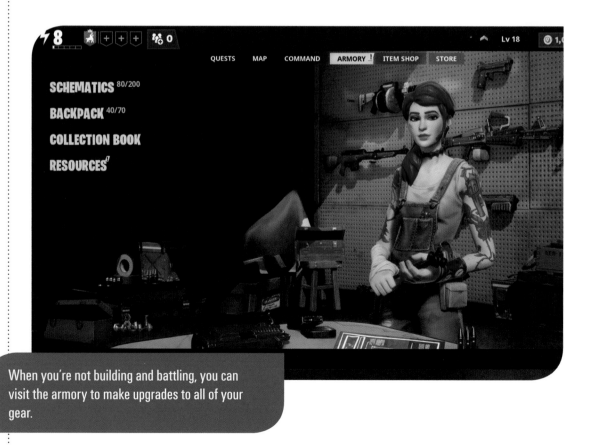

When you're not building and battling, you can visit the armory to make upgrades to all of your gear.

Making Friends

Save the World is designed to be a cooperative, or co-op, game. Whenever you start a new mission, you will see that up to three other players can join you. If you have friends who play the game, you can team up and battle alongside each other. This can make some of the tougher missions in Save the World a lot easier. It is also just a lot of fun to play with other people.

If your friends don't play Save the World, or if they aren't online when you want to play, you don't have to worry. The game will automatically try to find other players to join you when you start a mission. This can be a great way to find more players to add to your in-game friends list.

If you want to play missions by yourself, that's okay too. Things might be a little tougher, but with the right gear and enough practice, you can handle it.

all seem overwhelming at first. But with plenty of practice and a few tips to help you get started, you'll soon be saving the world with the best of them.

Epic Games continues to make changes and additions to Save the World, just as they do to *Fortnite*'s other modes. This means the game just keeps getting better and better, and there is always more to do. Any time is a great time to dive into Save the World mode, so let's get started!

Chapter 2

The Goals of the Game

When you start Save the World mode for the first time, you will be greeted with an animated scene explaining the basics of the game's story. Unlike Battle Royale mode, Save the World has a story that unfolds as you play. You will

over radio
We have survivors in danger. The storm's closing in!

Ray the robot is an important character in Save the World. She provides advice and guides you during missions.

Help Ramirez
○ Head inside the Bunker

You'll meet up with many computer-controlled characters while playing Save the World.

meet all kinds of wacky characters who will help you as you navigate your way through the game's many quests.

The basic storyline of the game is that mysterious storms have appeared all around the world. Most of the planet's people have disappeared. Worse yet, there are zombie-like monsters called husks wandering around. This all means that the world has become a very dangerous place. The surviving humans have started banding together to build bases and defend themselves against the husks. These people are also working to build storm shields, which create safe areas inside the deadly storms.

In Save the World, you are the leader of a group of survivors. Over the course of the game, you will build up your base and improve your defenses. You will also track down fellow survivors and heroes and bring them to your base, making your group even stronger.

To progress in Save the World, you will complete a series of quests. Each quest takes place in a different

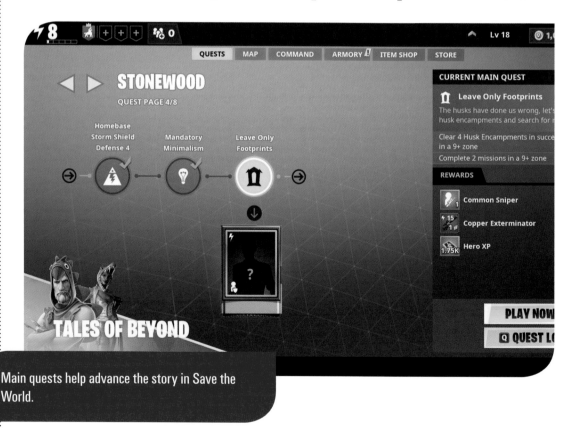

Main quests help advance the story in Save the World.

location and has slightly different goals. Sometimes you will need to defend your base for a certain amount of time as enemies continually attack. Other times you might need to find and rescue a certain number of survivors within a time limit. Or you might need to find certain items.

Additionally, there are various challenges you can complete as you play quests. For example, the game might ask you to defeat 500 enemies. Your total continues from quest to quest until you defeat all 500, and then you get a reward. These challenges are very similar to the daily and weekly challenges in Battle Royale.

For each quest or challenge you complete, you will be rewarded with a variety of very useful unlockable items. We will take a look at which kinds of items you can unlock in later chapters. However, you should know that everything you unlock by completing quests will make you and your base stronger. You will be able to defeat more powerful enemies and take on more difficult quests.

Playing through the early quests of Save the World is a great way to learn the basics of the game. Each quest will typically introduce a new aspect of the

Pay to Play

One of the reasons *Fortnite*'s Battle Royale mode has become so popular is that it is free for anyone to play. Save the World works differently. Like most video games, it requires a one-time purchase before you can get started.

Like Battle Royale, Save the World also offers a wide range of **microtransactions** to spend money on. You can purchase **skins** for your characters. You can also purchase new weapons and other gear to use in the game. All of these things cost V-bucks. You can earn small amounts of V-bucks by playing the game. You can also buy them with real money. Be careful if you choose to spend money on *Fortnite*'s in-game shop. Even though each item or skin might seem inexpensive, the costs can quickly add up if you buy multiple things. Also, you should always get your parents' permission before spending real money in *Fortnite*!

game. For example, the very first quest teaches you the basics of how to build. Others teach you how to craft and upgrade your weapons, or how to make your base stronger. In fact, many of the game's systems and features are not even available until you reach the quest that introduces them. (If you read about something in this book and can't find it in your own game, you probably haven't gotten to that quest yet!)

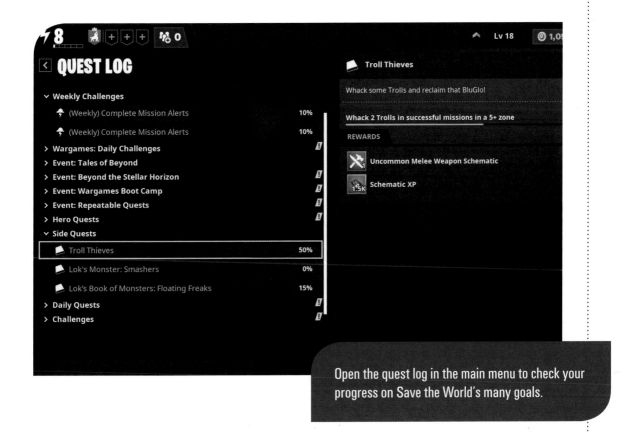

Open the quest log in the main menu to check your progress on Save the World's many goals.

There is a huge number of quests to complete in Save the World. The main storyline is divided into four main sections. In each one, you will visit a different part of the *Fortnite* world to build your base and fend off enemies. With each new area, the enemies grow more powerful, and the rewards get better. It will take a long time to finish all the quests in the main story. Even after you do, you'll have tons of side quests and challenges to beat.

Chapter 3

Gearing Up

One of the biggest keys to success in Save the World is making sure you have the right gear. Just like in Battle Royale, you will need to scavenge and gather supplies to fill your **inventory**. However, this process is far more complex in Save the World. Also, the items you gather will be stored permanently in your inventory. You do not have to start

You will find supplies hidden all over the place in Save the World's levels, so explore carefully.

SORTED BY RATING

MELEE WEAPONS

CRAFTING

BACKPACK 40/ 70

Rare | Melee Weapon

MIGHTY SLUGGER

Copper | Melee | Club

⚡ 15 ★

DPS 231.5

Club: Light. A simple baseball bat with a and knockback. Home Run: Heavy attack that will send enemies flying.

You can open up your backpack at any time to see what you're carrying and craft new gear.

from scratch like you do when you start a new match of Battle Royale. This means that you will eventually have a huge collection of weapons, traps, and other tools to help you fight off the husks.

Whenever you set off on a quest, you will find yourself on an area of land that is much smaller than the Battle Royale island. However, there will still be plenty of room to explore. Usually, you will have plenty of time to wander around before starting the quest's main objective. You should definitely take advantage of this time to gather as many resources as you can.

Like Battle Royale, you can use your mining tool to take apart almost anything in the game world. This will allow you to gather the three main building materials: wood, stone, and metal. These work exactly like they do in Battle Royale. However, as you destroy things with your mining tool, you will also collect a variety of crafting materials. These range from duct tape and planks to batteries and crystals. There is a huge range of materials to find. You should try to collect as much as you can carry, as they will all come in handy.

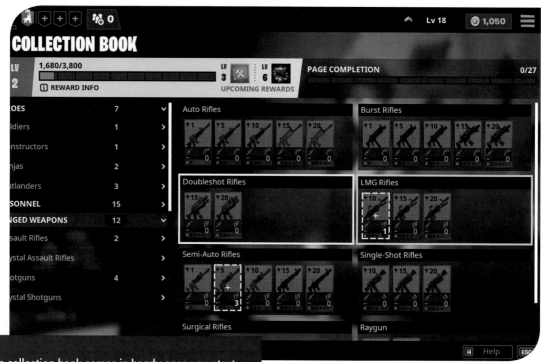

The collection book comes in handy once you start running out of space to carry new items.

You can carry a huge amount of stuff in Save the World. However, there are limits. You can only have 200 **schematics** at a time. You are also limited to 200 heroes, 200 survivors, and 200 defenders in your collection. (We'll talk more about these characters in the next chapter.)

So what do you do when you reach the limit? There will still be a lot of great new stuff to find and unlock after that, and you want to make sure you have space. Luckily, Save the World has a feature called the Collection Book. Here, you can donate unwanted schematics and characters to try to fill in a complete list. As you fill more spaces in the Collection Book, you will unlock various useful rewards. You can also go back to the collection book later to get back the things you have donated, for a price.

Mining isn't the only way to gather materials, ammo, and other useful items. As you search around the game's levels, you will find treasure chests, crates, and other containers filled with items you can loot. You will also run into various small challenges you can complete to earn items. For example, you might find a survivor who needs you to defeat some husks. Do so and you'll receive some supplies. Keep your eyes and ears open as you play, and you'll find all kinds of ways to increase your supplies.

In Save the World, you can craft your own weapons, ammo, and traps from the materials you find. To craft an item, you first need to find a schematic. Each item in the game has its own schematic. For example, there is a schematic that lets you build a basic assault rifle and another that lets you craft wall spike traps. Once you have the right schematic, you can craft its item as many times as you like, so long as you have the necessary materials. Each item requires a different combination and quantity of materials. The more you have in your backpack, the more items you can craft.

You will typically earn new schematics as rewards for completing quests. There are hundreds of them to unlock. At first, you will only have a few, which means your selection of weapons and traps will be limited. But eventually, you will have access to more gear than you know what to do with. You can pick and choose the weapons and traps you like best. You'll start to learn which ones work best against certain types of enemies or in specific situations.

Of course, the purpose of all this collecting and crafting is to make sure you have the tools to build forts and defeat enemies. In Save the World, most

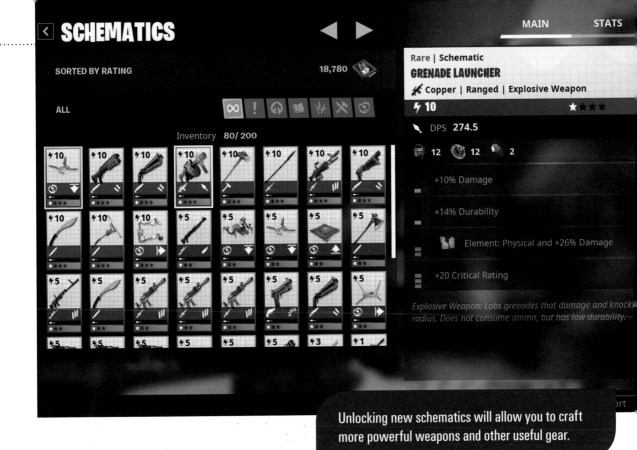

SCHEMATICS

SORTED BY RATING

18,780

ALL

Inventory 80/ 200

Rare | Schematic

GRENADE LAUNCHER

Copper | Ranged | Explosive Weapon

⚡ 10   ★ ★ ★

DPS **274.5**

12   12   2

+10% Damage

+14% Durability

Element: Physical and +26% Damage

+20 Critical Rating

Explosive Weapon: Lobs grenades that damage and knock
radius. Does not consume ammo, but has low durability.

Unlocking new schematics will allow you to craft
more powerful weapons and other useful gear.

quests require you to defend certain locations from
enemies for a period of time. Before the enemies
launch their attacks, you will get a chance to build up
your defenses. Like in Battle Royale, you can use wood,
stone, and metal to build walls, floors, ramps, and ceilings. These four shapes can be combined to create a
nearly limitless range of shapes. When you are building, try to make sure you defend against attacks from
all sides. You never know which direction enemies will
come from.

Time Until Extraction
10:39
288 520
EDIT G
PLACE TRAP
F3 EQUIP FLOOR TRAP
58
435
10
F
1
2

If you place your traps carefully, they can do a lot of damage to your enemies.

Also like in Battle Royale, you can add a variety of traps to your buildings. However, Save the World offers a much wider variety of traps to choose from. Some freeze enemies in their tracks. Others shoot out spikes to damage enemies. Different kinds of traps can be placed on walls, floors, or ceilings. Traps can make or break your chances of success on a quest. If you place your traps just right, they will take out most of the weaker enemies while you focus on the tougher ones.

Chapter 4

Colorful Characters

As you play through the storyline of Save the World, you will recruit dozens or even hundreds of characters to join you in the fight against the husks. They are divided into three categories: heroes, survivors, and defenders. Each one you find will make

Unlocking and upgrading heroes will allow you to take on tougher enemies in Save the World.

Heroes, survivors, and defenders can all be upgraded to make them more powerful. So can your schematics. As you play, you will earn experience points, or XP. There are different kinds of XP. One kind is used to upgrade heroes and defenders. Another is used for survivors. Another is only for schematics.

Once you have enough XP, you can choose to level up a character or schematic. Each time you level up, it will cost a larger amount of XP. Don't try to upgrade every character and schematic you get. Instead, it is better to save your XP for the characters and items you use most often.

your team stronger and allow you to take on tougher enemies and quests.

Heroes are playable characters. You will start out with just one hero: Rescue Trooper Ramirez. But soon, your team will expand to include many others. Before starting out on a quest, you will get to choose which hero you want to play as. Each one has a different name and appearance. However, there is more to the heroes than just looks. Different heroes have different **stats**. For example, some might have high health, but their shields take longer to **regenerate** after taking damage.

Each hero also has different abilities and perks. Abilities are special actions you can use while playing. For example, some heroes can teleport around the map or call giant robots to help them fight. Perks are bonuses that make the hero good at certain things. For example, some heroes have perks that make them do more damage when using specific kinds of weapons.

Heroes are divided into four categories called classes. The four classes are ninjas, constructors, soldiers, and outlanders. Each class has class-specific perks. For example, all ninjas can perform a second jump in mid-air. This allows them to jump very high. Constructors can add special armor to the structures they build. Soldiers have combat-focused abilities, while outlanders specialize in finding materials and gear. Different heroes within the same class usually have somewhat similar stats. However, their abilities and perks will vary, so be sure to examine them carefully. Experiment to see which heroes you like to play as.

Survivors are typically found hidden around the map when you are out on quests. You might find one hiding in an underground cave or tucked away behind

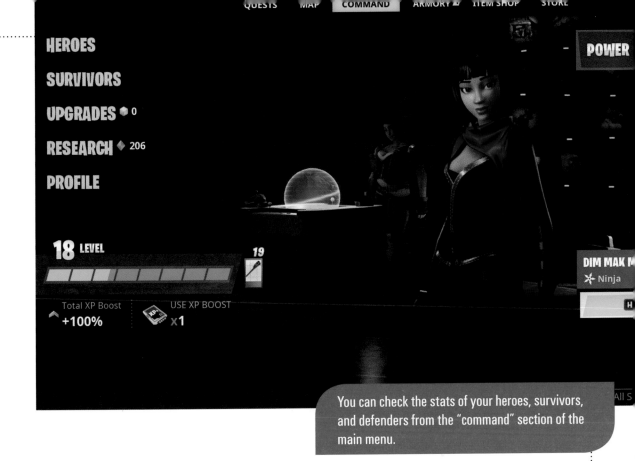

HEROES

SURVIVORS

UPGRADES ⬢ 0

RESEARCH ◆ 206

PROFILE

18 LEVEL

19

Total XP Boost
+100%

USE XP BOOST
x1

POWER

DIM MAK M
✴ Ninja

You can check the stats of your heroes, survivors, and defenders from the "command" section of the main menu.

a bookshelf in a house. Sometimes they will join you as soon as you find them. Other times, they will ask you to help them out first. In this case, you might need to defeat a few enemies or find a certain item before the survivor will join you.

Once survivors start joining you, you can assign them to squads. Each survivor in a squad offers a small boost to your character's stats. Different survivors offer different bonuses, so be sure to pick up as many of them as you can find.

Now that you know how to play, it's time to defeat some husks and Save the World!

You will also unlock characters called defenders as you play. Once you have some on your team, you can start building defender posts on your structures. Defender posts are special traps. Once you place one, you can select it and choose to summon one of your defenders. The defender will appear and help you fight off enemies.

Each defender can only use certain types of weapons. For example, some are able to use pistols, while others are limited to sniper rifles. You will need to give the defender a weapon and ammo from your own backpack. If you don't have the right weapon and you can't craft one, the defender won't be able to help you. Also, the defender can run out of ammo in the middle of a fight. If this happens, you will hear them call out to you. You will need to go to the defender and give them more ammo if you want them to continue fighting.

This might all sound like a lot to keep track of as you play. That's because it is! But the best way to learn is through practice. The more you play Save the World, the easier it will be to manage your team, upgrade the items you want, and complete quests. Good luck, and more importantly, have fun!

Glossary

craft (KRAFT) to make or build something

developers (dih-VEL-uh-purz) people who make video games or other computer programs

inventory (IN-vuhn-toh-ree) a list of the items your character is carrying

microtransactions (MYE-kroh-trans-ak-shuhns) things that can be purchased for a small amount of money within a video game or other computer program

regenerate (rih-JEN-uh-rayt) to be restored over time

scavenge (SKAV-uhnj) to search for useful items

schematics (skuh-MAT-iks) plans showing how something is built

skins (SKINZ) different appearances your character can take on in a video game

stats (STATS) numerical measurements

upgraded (UP-grayd-id) changed to make improvements

Find Out More

BOOKS

Cunningham, Kevin. *Video Game Designer*. Ann Arbor, Michigan: Cherry Lake Publishing, 2016.

Powell, Marie. *Asking Questions About Video Games*. Ann Arbor, Michigan: Cherry Lake Publishing, 2016.

WEBSITES

Epic Games—Fortnite
www.epicgames.com/fortnite/en-US/home
Check out the official *Fortnite* website.

Fortnite Wiki
https://fortnite.gamepedia.com/Fortnite_Wiki
This fan-made website offers up-to-date information on the latest additions to *Fortnite*.

Index

About the Author

Josh Gregory is the author of more than 150 books for kids. He has written about everything from animals to technology to history. A graduate of the University of Missouri–Columbia, he currently lives in Chicago, Illinois.